Life After Prozac

Life After Prozac

◆

A Memoir

Eva Del Bosque

iUniverse, Inc.
New York Lincoln Shanghai

Life After Prozac
A Memoir

iUniverse, Inc.

For information address:
iUniverse, Inc.
2021 Pine Lake Road, Suite 100
Lincoln, NE 68512
www.iuniverse.com

This book is sold with the understanding that it is purely personal philosophy. Please consult your physician before making any lifestyle and /or health changes. The author and publisher expressly disclaim any negative reaction directly or indirectly attributable to the use or application of any advice, information or suggestions in this book.

Photo Credit: A. Brandt

First iUniverse edition 2004.

www.lifeafterprozac.com

ISBN: 0-595-32256-5

Printed in the United States of America

With love and gratitude,
To Ann-Mari and Alfredo.

Contents

Acknowledgements

Thank you to all my friends, family and co-workers for their generous support. A special thanks to:

Healing Earth Resources
Heidi L. Schumann
Walter D. Street, IV
Andrew and William (at Compufind)
MiMi Sundeen
and
iUniverse

Introduction

"When the student is ready, the master appears."

—*Buddhist proverb*

Got a problem? Pop a pill.

I took Prozac for the better part of 12 years. Was that really necessary? Once I started, it was hard to stop. I didn't know what to do, and doctors weren't much help either. I was afraid. Afraid of the unknown.

Prozac may help some people, it may have helped me. Unfortunately, I got hooked. The media and medical establishment like to sell you a bill of goods: You're sick (i.e. depressed, have anxiety), take this pill, and you're good to go.

I chose to buy into this pop culture philosophy.

A week after starting Prozac, I felt like a new woman, able to jump off tall buildings in a single bound. I felt poised, confident and ready to take on the world.

"Aboundanza!" I shouted to my father. He was unimpressed.

On cloud nine, I told my mother the doctor's diagnosis: a chemical imbalance and a genetic predisposition.

I was the weakest link. She wasn't happy.

I felt like a million dollars and couldn't understand why she disapproved. Thankfully, she never bought into the diagnosis hook, line and sinker.

However, I felt a sense of relief that a doctor found out was wrong with me.

The truth is, there is nothing inherently wrong with me.

Yes, I get depressed. I have problems. Problems are opportunities.

I don't have all the answers.

My Uncle Frank says, "All the answers are within you."

If you think you're defective and an authority figure tells you such, you're toast.

A recent college graduate, I was having difficulties living in the real world. Away at school, I was in a protective cocoon. A grown-up reality was a shock to my system. My life was out of balance. Who has it all figured out in their twenties?

I was dejected, not defective.

Life can be frustrating; life can be beautiful-life is what you make it. My life isn't perfect, but it's real. Today, I lead an authentic life, filled with ups and downs, and a happy middle ground.

Mom and Prozac

A doctor said I should see a psychiatrist. He said I was too anxious. We had reached the end of the line. Like Alice, I was about to go through the looking-glass.

The waiting room was not crowded. The receptionist goes home. The doctor circled the room. He was confused. I should have taken that as a sign and left the building.

Instead, a twelve-year saga began.

The psychiatrist said I had a chemical imbalance. My neurons weren't kissing. I was charmed by his analogy. He highly recommended a new drug called Prozac. He said it would lessen my anxiety, which is a by-product of depression. Suddenly, I was a punch line in a Woody Allen movie.

The year was 1988 and Prozac was new on the market.

I hesitated. He said I might have to take it for years. I had doubts. He said therapy wasn't necessary. He said to sleep on it and come back tomorrow.

The next day I signed on the dotted line. He planted the seed. I happily watered it.

Years later, I was still on Prozac. (The doctor left town six weeks after we met). I read in a magazine that depression was a mental illness.

I told my mother I took Prozac because my neurons weren't kissing and was mentally ill.

She said, "You're not mentally ill." Bless Ann-Mari.

Having an Advocate is Good Therapy

- Pop Culture Reference: *Girl Interrupted (1999).*

The Turning Point

I had a feeling I wanted to stop taking Prozac. This romance had been going on for years. A few months prior, my doctor suggested I see a pharmacologist and a therapist.

The pharmacologist had recently recommended I up my dosage from 20mg to 30, because I wasn't feeling good.

I did, and felt better. But was sleepy. I was in school and was too drowsy to study.

I mentioned to the therapist that I was thinking of giving up Prozac for good.

He was against the idea. He was afraid. He said because I was in school, I should wait.

Shortly thereafter, I felt a vague dissatisfaction.

The pharmacologist had already taken two minutes to decide to up my dosage from 20mg to 30, to the tune of $250.00 dollars, charged to my insurance company.

I thought, "What's next? 40mg? 50mg? And then the loony bin? And I'm *Girl Interrupted*, and have electric shock treatment like *One Flew Over the Cuckoo's Nest?*"

Game over.

Taking Control Is Good Therapy

- Pop Culture: *One Flew Over the Cuckoo's Nest* (1975).

4

Stuck On Prozac Island

o o o o o o o o o o o o o o o o o o o o o o o o o o o o o o o o o o o

"Sine qua non"

—Indispensable

I struggled with how to get off Prozac Island. I didn't think I could survive without it. I tried Zoloft, St. John's Wort and going cold turkey, always returning to my old stand-by.

After 12 years of this candy colored merry-go round, I gave up Prozac for good. Despite many tears, sadness and anxiety it's the best thing I've ever done.

To be happy, focus on what you want.

Change Is Good Therapy

* Pop Culture: Johnson, Spencer. *Who Moved My Cheese?* New York: G. P. Putnam's Sons, 1998.

About Prozac

There are many good books written about Prozac, pro and con. Knowledge is power. If you go to a library or a bookstore, you can learn a lot. Get acquainted with the current research.

Books of interest:

1. Peter D. Kramer. *Listening to Prozac.* New York: Penguin Books, 1993.
2. Lou Martinoff. *Plato, not Prozac!* New York: HarperCollins, 1999.
3. Joseph Glenmullen. *Prozac Backlash.* New York: Touchstone, 2001.

Knowledge Is Good Therapy

- Pop Culture: Bloomfield, Harold. *Making Peace with Your Past.* New York: HarperCollins, 2000.

Three Ways To Heal

My favorite ways to heal:

Exercise

I like to swim, dance or walk. When swimming, troubles wash away. Ideas and solutions float to the surface.

Meditate

To meditate, I get quiet, acknowledge my thoughts and let them go. Or, I reflect on what comes up. A solution or path of action may appear.

Pray

I pray for strength to handle whatever comes my way. I pray to improve my life. I like to creatively visualize my new world. What I'll be wearing, what I'll be doing, and whom I'll be with.

Healing Is Good Therapy

- Pop Culture: Gawain,Shatki. *Creative Visualization*. Novato, CA: Nataraj Publishing, 1995.

Make A List

I like to make a list every day. Having a list grounds me. We all lead busy lives and it's easy to be distracted from goals, dreams and desires.

When writing a list, I learn what's important, what's necessary, and what's optional.

Creating a list is like making your own roadmap. And like kindness, it doesn't cost anything.

1. Read the newspaper
2. Mail bills
3. Eat lunch
4. Go swimming
5. Be grateful for being alive

Making A List Is Good Therapy

- Pop Culture: Carlson, Richard. *Don't Sweat the Small Stuff...and It's All Small Stuff.* New York: Hyperion, 1997.

Develop A Routine

Here's how I start my day.

1. Shower.
2. Read the paper.
3. Eat breakfast.

Life can be stressful. I like to prepare by taking good care of myself. Before taking a shower, I meditate or do a few minutes of Reiki. (A method of healing. Reiki means "universal life energy").

Reading the paper grounds me to the outside world, putting me in touch with current events. Sometimes I buy the USA Today, or one of the Chicago papers. Another favorite is the Wall Street Journal.

Food is fuel for the body. Treat your body well and it will reciprocate. After breakfast, I'm ready for a hectic, crazy day as a clerk on the trading floor.

Routine Is Good Therapy

- Pop Culture: Horan, Paula. *Empowerment through Reiki*. Twin Lakes, WI: Lotus Light Publications, 1990.

Mission Statement

Write yourself a mission statement. Once mine was for a *Summer of Love*. I learned about life, love and romance. What's important to you? How would you like to spend your days and nights?

My current mission statement is—*Write an uplifting, healing and entertaining book, Life After Prozac.*

Create a mission statement for the summer, a season, or for the rest of your life. Let your statement summarize and be a guiding force for creating the life of your dreams. A mission statement is an opportunity to clarify who you are, and what you want.

Ask yourself the following:

1. What would you like to accomplish?
2. What are you for?
3. Against?

Mission statement samples:

1. *To attain Inner Peace and Prosperity*
2. *Winter of Joy*
3. *Spring of Happiness*

Mission Statements' Are Good Therapy

• Pop Culture Reference: Feinstein, David, and Krippner, Stanley. *Personal Mythology.* New York: Jeremy P. Tarcher, 1998.

Mentor

What is a mentor?

According to the dictionary, a person looked upon for wise advice and guidance.

I have a trader friend named Julie. We've been friends for years. She's a little older than I, and as a result, has more life experience. Julie has taught me to be assertive, to stay positive and to never give up. She's concerned about my well-being, dreams and frustrations. Julie likes me for me. One day it dawned on me—I don't need to find a mentor. I have one.

I feel very fortunate and grateful to have a mentor. Being grateful allows you to feel humble and connected to humanity. Being grateful lifts your spirits, allowing you to be optimistic about the future.

Is there someone in your life you consider a mentor: a teacher, a favorite uncle, or a co-worker?

Often I marvel at my supervisors who are calm under pressure. The trading floor can get intense, traders yelling, runners running and orders flying through the air.

Write three things you're grateful for:

1. The sun.
2. The moon.
3. Julie, a shining star.

Mentors Are Good Therapy

• Pop culture: Ryan, M. J. *Attitudes of Gratitude.* Berkeley, CA: Conari Press, 1999.

Develop Your Power Base

Live in a place you can afford, in a neighborhood you like.

Have a job that offers you benefits, such as good medical insurance, dental and 401-K. Find a doctor or medical group that is to your liking and convenient.

These are all ingredients to help you establish your power base. Once your basic needs are taken care of, you can set goals to challenge yourself. Develop your power base and go from there.

A Power Base Is Good Therapy

- Pop Culture Reference: Chopra, Deepak. *The Seven Spiritual Laws of Success.* San Rafael, CA: New World Library, 1994.

Location

The key to real estate is, location, location, location.

When I was fifteen, I worked for a market research firm. We called and interviewed people all over America and wrote our answers in longhand.

My parents were divorced since I was ten, but once I asked my father if he would pick me up after work.

His reply, "Find a job closer to home."

The key to life is, location, location, location.

I like living near work, the Laundromat, the health club, my friends, the movies and grocery stores. Everything is a walk, a bus, or an "L" train away. This adds significantly to my quality of life.

Location Is Good Therapy

- Pop Culture Reference: Linn, Denise. *Sacred Space*. New York: Ballantine Books, 1995.

Higher Education

o o o o o o o o o o o o o o o o o o o o o o o o o o o o o o o o o
"Follow your Bliss"

—Joseph Campbell

Education is something no one can take away from you.

I took one class towards my Master's Degree and decided it wasn't for me. Taking an introductory class was a great way to learn about the program before committing two years of my life and thousands of dollars. Academia isn't for everyone. There are many roads to Rome. Find the way that suits you best.

1. What work activity do you like best?
2. Least?
3. What do you see yourself doing five years from now?

Self-knowledge is Good Therapy

• Pop Culture Reference: Trungpa, Chogyam. *SHAMBHALA, The Sacred Path of the Warrior.* Boston, MA: Shambhala Publications, 1984.

Two Tostadas to Go, Please

I worked the last Census as an enumerator. In the early evening, I went knocking on doors asking people their race, how many occupants in their home and how much money did they make.

For fifteen dollars an hour, this was a good part-time job. In a booth at a Burger King, our supervisor would check our completed surveys for accuracy. Sometimes I would buy a cheeseburger after work. One night I chose to go to a Mexican restaurant instead.

The owner Mr. Z, worked behind the bar. I ordered two tostadas to go, and introduced myself. Told him I was Swedish and Mexican. I also sold real estate. Mr. Z asked to see some investment property listings.

A real estate relationship was born. He never did buy an apartment building. Instead, Mr. Z retired. My broker and I sold his building, including the restaurant. One year later, I earned a check for more than half my regular salary.

Get a license. Take a class, go back to school; you never know where it will lead you.

Getting A License Is Good Therapy

- Coelho, Paul. *The Alchemist.* London: HarperCollins Publishers, 1995.

Good Neighbor

My Mother once had a neighbor named Bradley Goodman. I was young and looking to find my way in the world.

I met Bradley when I moved back home after college. He would make a pot of tea and as we talked, Bradley hand painted the faces of miniature harlequin dolls. He had more than one job.

One day, as we were talking about my career misadventures, Bradley offered this nugget of wisdom, "Sometimes you have to work a lot of different jobs, finding what's not right for you in order to find what is." That has definitely been my career path.

1. Has a neighbor been helpful to you?
2. Make a list of all the jobs you've had.
3. Describe your dream job.

Good Neighbors Are Good Therapy

- Pop Culture: Richmond, Lewis. *Work as a Spiritual Practice*. New York: Broadway Books, 1999.

Take A Class

Classes are a great way to expand your knowledge. I've taken classes in writing, real estate and kundalini yoga. Knowledge is power. My mother has often said, "If you learn just one thing, it's a success."

Sometimes I've learned a lot, and sometimes 'just one thing'.

Take a class, and learn something today.

1. What would you like to learn about?
2. How could a class improve your life?
3. Why is it important to keep learning?

Classes Are Good Therapy

- Pop Culture Reference: Canfield, Jack, Hansen, Mark Victor, Gardner, Bud. *Chicken Soup For The Writer's Soul.* Deerfield Beach, FL. Health Communications, 2000.

Writing Class

I took a writing class at the Newberry Library. I learned about the art of writing, about my fellow students and myself.

One day, the teacher asked us to recall two stories from our childhood. I chose to tell one about Mom and one about Dad.

Growing up, my mother would often make me tea and toast for breakfast. Hurriedly I'd wash, dress, and eat the toast without drinking any tea, since it was very hot.

After I had schoolbooks in hand, my mother would ask, "Did you drink your tea?" I'd always reply, "No, it's too hot," and run down the stairs.

I had read an article about a child actress in the newspaper. She had gone to acting school. I told my mother I wanted to take acting lessons. After inquiring about two schools, Jack and Jill Players was chosen. She was pleased with the conversation she had with one of the teachers.

Even though my parents were divorced, my mother assigned my father with the task of taking me to and from acting class on Saturday afternoons.

After class, driving home Dad would say, "I don't know why I have to pick you up. You're never going to be an actress anyway."

The class gave me a round of applause.

The more someone is in pain, the louder they strike out. Dad was in pain. His father was probably in pain. And so on.

Writing Is Good Therapy

- Pop Culture: Evans, Patricia. *The Verbally Abusive Relationship*. Holbrook, MA: Adams Media Corporation, 1996.

Family

On the way to a second-hand store, my five-year old niece asked me, "Auntie Eva, why aren't you married?"

I told her I had been married, but my husband wasn't happy, so we got a divorce.

"What was his name?"

"Fred."

"Isn't that your Dad's name?"

"Very good. My dad's name was Alfred, your grandfather."

My sister was in the driver's seat, with her three children, ages eight, five and four in the back seat. The chorus began.

"Are you going to get married again?"

"Can I be the flower girl?"

"Can I meet him before you get married?"

I assured them they were all invited; they could be flower girls' and their little brother, the ring bearer. And yes, they could meet him, as soon as I do.

I said they could "marry" themselves if they wanted.

"I want to marry a tree."

"I want to marry a leaf."

"I want to marry my shadow."

Finally, my four-year old nephew said, "I want to marry my penis."

Family Is Good Therapy

• Pop Culture: Leman, Kevin. *Birth Order Book*. Grand Rapids, MI: Baker Books, 2004.

Marriage

My cousin is getting married.

Weddings are fun. The invitations, the showers, the Elvis impersonator. Walking down the aisle with my father to Roy Orbison's *Pretty Woman.* My wedding was very nice. Marriage was the hard part.

He was in a hurry to move in, in a hurry to get married and in a hurry to get divorced.

As kids, our father would take my sister and I for ice cream at Thirty-one Flavors, but we could only have one scoop. Dad was a one-scoop kind of guy. He believed in moderation.

While dating, Fred took me to *Taste of Chicago.* He had a massive amount of red tickets. I had chicken and pizza and ice cream and a candied apple, to go. Never had one of those. Not in my one-scoop childhood.

He also he gave me candles, clothes and lots of attention.

Maybe I was in a hurry too.

Fred was a sweet and gentle soul. The marriage lasted a year.

Life Is Good Therapy

• Pop Culture: Reiser, Paul. *Couplehood.* New York: Bantam Books, 1994.

Divorce

Getting divorced is difficult. Life can be difficult. Seems you've barely opened the presents, sent the thank-you notes, stocked up on dishes and cutlery, big bowls and small bowls and it's over.

Someone suggested his sixteen-year old daughter was to blame. She moved in a few months after we wed. There wasn't a lot of discussion. She didn't want to live at home anymore, that was it.

I will be eternally grateful this teen-ager moved in with us. Why? She shed some light on the marriage, it wasn't working and it wasn't her fault.

As much as I didn't want to break up, it is better than staying in an unhappy, unhealthy situation.

A few weeks after we separated, I had two wisdom teeth removed.

After he moved out, the energy in the apartment lifted. I knew I was better off. An extraction is painful.

Rituals Are Good Therapy

- Pop Culture: Friedman, Sonya. *Men are just Desserts*. New York: Warner Books, 1983.

Marriage II

Once, I told a doctor I felt better on Prozac but didn't know why.

His reply, "When you remarry, you'll be happy."

He was from Pakistan, and maybe this was true in his culture. However, filling a prescription at the local pharmacy for "One happy marriage" is not an option.

Does marriage equal happiness, making Prozac obsolete?

Being happy is a choice, not a marital status. Years later, I've yet to remarry. It's easy to look to marriage or to anything, as a road to nirvana. From my experience, marriage brings a whole new set of problems/opportunities.

Find the benefits whatever your marital status—each has it's own rewards. Two happy people make for a better marital foundation. Choose to be happy today.

1. What brings you happiness?
2. What can you do to increase the joy in your life?
3. Are you happy? If not, why?

Choosing To Be Happy Is Good Therapy

• Pop Culture: Kaufman, Barry Neil. *Happiness Is a Choice*. New York: Fawcett Columbine, 1991.

Establish Yourself First

Establish yourself first, is one of my favorite mantras. You need to be able to walk before you can run. Growing up, my Dad would say, "Establish yourself first." I didn't understand what he meant. Now that he's passed on, I know exactly what he means.

He means develop yourself mentally, physically and professionally, before you get married. Have a career, achieve some success, take care of yourself and know who you are. Then, you're free to start a family. You'll be on solid ground.

1. Where would you like to be a year from now?
2. In five years?
3. Ten years?

Establishing Yourself First is Good Therapy

• Pop Culture: *Sweet Home Alabama,* (2002).

Mom

I love my Mom. Sometimes she drives me crazy.

Someone once asked me what my mother was good at. My Mother is good at many things. She's a great listener, a short-order cook, funny, smart, an artist, painter, decorator, teacher, daughter, mother, grandmother, friend and confidant extraordinaire. My mother is interested in many things.

She has *joie de vivre*.

When I had a problem in college, she was there for me, always lending an ear.

When I had my tonsils removed, she was there for me.

When I got a divorce, she was there for me.

When I felt I needed to go back on Prozac, and didn't have the money, she was there for me and took me out to dinner.

When I was up all night, sick with the stomach flu, she was there for me, a middle-of-the night phone call away.

Some people have told me they were envious, wished they were as good friends with their mother.

Sometimes, Mom gets on my last nerve, but mostly she teaches me about compassion. My sister Ingrid says, "It's a mother's job to irritate you."

No one loves you like your mother.

Compassion is Good Therapy

- Pop Culture: Ruiz, Don Miguel. *The Four Agreements*. San Rafael, CA: Amber-Allen Publishing, Inc, 1997.

Make Your Life a Work Of Art

o o o o o o o o o o o o o o o o o o o o o o o o o o o o o o o o

"There's no one in the world just like you."

—*Ann-Marism*

Inspiring words from my mother, the artist. If you want to paint your walls yellow, pink or chartreuse, do it. It's your life.

Dress, wear your hair and decorate your home as you please.

Once, a co-worker asked me, "Why do you cut your bangs?"

My reply, "It makes me happy."

It's your responsibility to make your life fun, interesting and enjoyable. When you're happy, other people pick up on your positive vibrations and it's contagious. Being depressed is catching also. Be like an artist and make your life a work of art.

Being An Artist Is Good Therapy

- Pop Culture: SARK. *The Bodacious Book of Succulence.* New York: Fireside, 1998.

Be Your Own Mother

Learn to nurture yourself. Being your own mother is about the little things and the big things. Encourage yourself. Get proper rest. Buy yourself nice clothes. Get regular check-ups, medical and dental.

Act on your ideas. Believe in yourself, your feelings and dreams.

Plan for the future. Take a personal or vacation day when you need one. Take a nap when you're tired. Buy yourself a toy.

A good parent works their way out of a job. Be your own parent.

Becoming Your Own Parent Is Good Therapy

- Pop Culture Reference: De Angelis, Barbara. *Secrets About Life Every Woman Should Know.* New York: Hyperion, 1999.

Alfredo (1933–1998)

I miss my father. My ego misses him. I want him to be my mirror. Tell me how pretty I am.

I want to say, "Look how much money I made in real estate. How you like me now?"

"Finally!" he'd say. "Where's my cut?"

I'd look shocked.

Then he'd burst into a huge smile.

"That's great," he'd say.

Often, we don't appreciate people until they're gone. Dad is in my heart. I know he just loves me now. His spirit is alive and well.

Life is a gift. People are here. And one day they're gone. Sometimes you get a warning. Sometimes you don't. Treasure the moment.

1. Do you miss someone who has passed on?
2. Write them a letter.
3. Write a letter from them to you. Or create a dialogue.

Happy Memories Are Good Therapy

• Pop Culture: *The Godfather* (1972).

Dreams

Dad loved people, parties, food and fun. After his death, he visited me in my dreams.

It was a gathering of people. I stepped into the buffet line. There was my father.
"Dad, you had us all fooled, we thought you were dead."
"Love doesn't die, it just changes form," he replied.

1. Keep a dream journal.
2. What do your dreams mean to you?
3. Share your dream with another, or write a story.

Dreams are Good Therapy

- Pop Culture: Epel, Naomi. *Writers Dreaming*. New York: Vintage Books, 1993.

Dad And Death

I was downtown, near the Harold Washington Library. There's an "L" stop at the library. I was street level and looking up. There on the platform, was an elderly man.

He had an English cap on, like Dad used to wear after they removed one of his eyes. Like Dad, he wore a waist length jacket. Like Dad, he wasn't very tall or short. I kept looking at him. It was a sunny day in Chicago. "Maybe that's my father," I thought.

It's common to imagine you've seen a dearly departed. Write a story or tell a friend.

Observance is Good Therapy

• Stone, Richard. *The Healing Art of Storytelling.* New York, Hyperion, 1996.

Another Day, Another Dream

It was a party. I went to the basement. Standing with a group of people near the beverage table, in a snazzy black leather jacket, was Dad. I didn't recognize him.

"Remember me?" he said, smiling.

"Hi, Dad! How are you?"

He had both of his eyes. He was happy. And happy to see me.

Remembrance is Good Therapy

• Pop Culture: Kubler-Ross,Elizabeth, Kessler, David. New York: *Life Lessons.* Scribner, 2000.

Ignorance

Someone asked me how old my Dad was when he died.

"Sixty-five," I replied.

"That's too young."

I disagree. My cousin Avery died in his twenties. Neither died in vain. Each led full lives. They both loved and were loved back. They touched my heart and countless others. It doesn't matter how long you live, it matters *how* you lived. Dad wasn't perfect. He could be difficult. But I love my Dad, and would give anything to have him back.

Having Grace Is Good Therapy

- Pop Culture: Beattie, Melody. *The Lessons of Love*. New York: HarperCollins, 1994.

Friends

I enjoy having many friends. Work friends, neighbor friends, sister friends, movie friends and family friends.

My Uncle Frank says, "You're lucky if you have a few good friends in your lifetime." There's a special chemistry you experience with a good friend.

My Dad once said, "Marrieds stick with marrieds and singles stick with singles." After my divorce I understood what he meant.

Danny

Years ago, Danny and I worked at a record store on Rush Street. It had four floors of music and a video department in the basement.

Danny now manages a coffeehouse and is a haircutter. One day, I was showing some apartments and had a few minutes between showings, and found Danny at the coffee shop.

We quickly caught up with old times and new. Sometimes I try to write a few words in his shop. Usually we end up talking about relationships and the other mysteries of the universe.

I'm always in a good mood when I see Danny. We'll talk about my book.

He'll say, "I'm writing it for you!"

"Thanks for your help, Danny!" I'll say.

Danny and I laugh a lot. We see the highest good in each other.

Nina And Billy

It can get awfully cold in Chicago in the wintertime. That's when it's great to have friends and neighbors' like Nina and Billy. Billy is a computer wizard. Nina works in finance. We live in the same apartment building.

Billy sold me my first computer and taught me how to use it. When I wanted to highlight my hair, Nina helped me.

They're also excellent cooks. Often they invite me to dinner. Baked salmon with cous cous. Shrimp Scampi with pasta and red sauce. Vegetable ravioli soup. I love their cooking and their company. Good neighbors are good friends to have.

Janis

I met Janis when we were both extras on the set of *Mad Dog and Glory*. She likes to tease me that she's a friend of the producer, but I made the final cut in the movie.

Janis manages *The Hungry Brain*, a bar on Belmont. Janis is kind and funny, a fabulous listener and better than any therapist I've ever had.

Good Friends Are Good Therapy

* Pop Culture: Seinfeld, Jerry. *SeinLanguage*. New York: Bantam Books, 1993.

Always Have Something to Look Forward to

One Monday, I felt lighter and happier at work. The day sailed by-nothing got me down. I was going to see my friend Janis. We had made plans to meet at a Thai restaurant, to celebrate my birthday.

We both made the observation that our day went better because we had something to look forward to. A movie, dinner with friends—always have something to look forward to. Life is short-take time to celebrate.

Looking Forward Is Good Therapy

- Pop Culture: *Joe Cocker Live,* Capitol Records (1990).

Aunt Joan

When you're younger, you think you and your relatives will live forever. My Aunt Joan passed away a few years ago. She was a lively, talented, sensitive woman. Sometimes I feel her presence. Sometimes she visits me in my dreams.

My favorite affirmation she gave me is, *"You have beauty and brains."* Words can hurt, words can inspire. We all crave recognition.

Aunt Joan told me from an early age I was like her, sensitive.

After she died I thought about what it means to be sensitive. To have great feelings is not a bad thing. Some people are more sensitive than others. One must learn to manage one's feelings. Develop a thick skin. Take extra good care of yourself. Being sensitive can be a burden or a blessing. Many great artists were sensitive. Van Gogh. Janis Joplin and Marilyn Monroe.

We are the sum of our choices. I feel fortunate to be sensitive, and grateful I had an Aunt who showed me the way. Are you extra sensitive? It's a gift, and so was my Aunt Joan.

Awareness Is Good Therapy

- Pop Culture: Van Praagh, James. *Talking to Heaven*. New York: Dutton, 1997.

Crazy

o o o o o o o o o o o o o o o o o o o o o o o o o o o o o o o o o o
Insane
Crazy
Loco
Loony
Kooky
Cosmic

Years ago, I was distraught, feeling out of control. I wanted to escape, run away. From life. From problems.

I thought checking into a hospital was a viable option. I had insurance. I had doctors to admit me. It would be like a mini-vacation.

Only, my problems would still be my problems when I got out.

Only, it would be one week later.

Only, I would have the added stigma of being in the hospital for my "mental" problems.

I wasn't crazy. Just afraid.

I had "coping with life" problems. How to handle life. How to be happy. How to live with setbacks. How to bounce back. How to achieve peace of mind.

Figure out what you want. Then slowly, methodically, step by step-GO FOR IT. Only you know what's best for you.

Be your own best healer.

Living Life Is Good Therapy

- Pop Culture: Anderson, Walter. *The Confidence Course.* New York: HarperPerennial, 1997.

Courage

o o o o o o o o o o o o o o o o o o o o o o o o o o o o o o o
"You must do the thing you think you cannot do."

—*Eleanor Roosevelt*

I'd wanted to write a book for a long time. I was afraid. Somehow, I summoned the courage. Took a few writing classes, did research, talked about it and bought a used laptop, and started tapping away. For once in my life I felt a deep sense of fulfillment.

1. Is there something you'd like to do?
2. What's stopping you?
3. What steps do you need to take, to make this goal a reality?

Achievement Is Good Therapy

• Pop Culture: Osho. *Courage.* New York: St. Martin's Griffin, 1999.

Get Excited

Once I discovered how much I like to write, I became excited.

Try different things, until you learn what interests you. What makes your heart pound?

When you have enthusiasm, it's contagious. It carries you over the rough spots. Makes you want to get out of bed each day and greet the world with a happy dance.

1. Take a class.
2. Learn a new skill.
3. Visit a foreign country.

Enthusiasm Is Good Therapy

- Pop Culture: Stoddard, Alexandra. *The Art of the Possible.* William Morrow & Company, 1995.

Baby Steps

Dream big. Dream about what kind of life you'd like. Dreaming gives you an opportunity to lead the life you've always wanted. To travel, change careers, or start a family. Whatever is important to you. If you can dream it, you can be it.

Goals are what you set in order to make your dreams come true. Set reasonable goals and a timeline for your dreams to manifest.

Rome wasn't built in a day. Break your goals into even smaller portions. If you want to write a book, start by writing a page at a time.

Break that down even further by writing just a few words. Take baby steps. In the movie *What About Bob?* it's all about taking baby steps to change your life. Make a phone call about that class you're interested in. Go to the library and do some research. It's your life. Start dreaming.

1. Dream big
2. Set manageable goals
3. Take baby steps

Baby Steps Are Good Therapy

- Pop Culture: *What About Bob?* (1991).

Life Mapping

"An unexamined life is not worth living."

—Socrates

A powerful tool for self-knowledge is life mapping. Write down a timeline of significant events in your life. Life transitions such as first job, graduation, moving, and marriage. What happened and why? Do this with smaller events, also.

Is there anything you would do differently? Do you see any patterns? By understanding the story of your life, you're in a better position to create your future. Let the past serve you as a guide.

1. Create a time-line of events. Look for patterns.
2. Try career mapping.
3. Romance mapping.

Life Mapping Is Good Therapy

• Pop Culture: de Mello, Anthony. *Awareness.* New York: Image, 1992.

A Few Good Words

Death is inevitable. Write your own obituary. Go to the end of your life and go backwards in time. For example;

> Eva died in her sleep at the age of 99. She wrote many books, including *Life After Prozac*. She and her husband were married for over fifty years. They had two children, many grandchildren and great-grandchildren.

This is a helpful exercise to help you think about your goals and what you want to accomplish. Take time to go back to the future today.

Words Are Good Therapy

• Pop Culture: Fitzgerald, F. Scott. *The Great Gatsby*. New York: Scribner Paperback Fiction, 1995.

Do Nothing

We live in a busy world. Work, children, cell phones, faxes, meetings, chores and errands. The list of things to do is endless. I'm a big list-maker. Sometimes I put the list aside and do nothing. Doing nothing gives your mind, soul and body a break.

Constant busyness is a form of abuse. Understand you are a human being, not a human doing. Nourish yourself. Take a walk or sit in a favorite chair. Relax. After time spent doing nothing, I feel clearer, about who I am and what I want. I feel refreshed and energized, ready to continue life and its challenges, dreams and diversions.

Give yourself permission to do nothing.

1. Set aside an afternoon or day.
2. Get a massage. Relax.
3. Just breathe.

Doing Nothing Is Good Therapy

- Pop Culture: Brewer, Sarah. *Simply Relax.* Berkeley, CA: Ulysses Press, 2000.

Saying No

Sometimes the most loving thing you can say to someone is "no". I often find it difficult saying no, because I'm afraid. Afraid people won't like me if I say no to their requests.

Over time I've learned it's OK to say no. I might be busy, have other plans or just not interested. I like myself more if I honor my own needs first. I have no control over other people liking me. The "disease to please" is a 'dis' ease with your self.

If you're unsure about a request, say so. Whether it's a date, a new job, or a vacation destination, give yourself time to decide.

Honor yourself and your choices. When you respect yourself, others will usually respect you.

1. Saying no is OK.
2. Saying you will "think about it" is acceptable.
3. What is stopping you from saying no?

Saying No Is Good Therapy

- Pop culture: Breitman, Patti and Hatch, Connie. *How to Say No Without Feeling Guilty.* New York: Broadway Books, 2000.

43

Set Boundaries

Early one morning in the washroom, a co-worker asked me to carry her purse back to the office.

"OK," I replied.

I was miffed. I didn't want to be carrying anyone's handbag.

A few months later, in an elevator filled to the brim, again she handed me her purse.

"You take it," I said. Suddenly, several eyes were staring at me as if I had said a bad word.

Later, I took her aside, and said, "I didn't want to carry your purse since: I have my own purse to carry, I don't want to be held responsible, and if there is a problem, management won't want to get involved."

Sometimes you have to draw the line, set boundaries. This encounter taught me to be assertive.

She never asked me to carry her purse again. We're still friends.

Once people know your limits, you're free to enjoy life. It's a win-win situation.

Assert your independence and draw the line.

1. If someone is your friend, they'll respect you.
2. If someone is your enemy, they'll respect you.
3. Most importantly, you'll respect yourself.

Boundaries Are Good Therapy

• Pop Culture: Katherine, Anne. *Where to Draw the Line*. New York: Fireside, 2000.

Healthy Days

I am eligible for six sick days a year. I hesitate using them.

The last time I called in sick, I was in physical pain and figured it was necessary.

Also, I would be a martyr if I didn't get some rest.

Returning to work, I was greeted by the following "We missed you," "Good to hear your voice" "Hope you're feeling better." Did I ever state the exact nature of my illness? No, because it was more information than anyone needed to know.

Once, I hadn't been feeling well for a few days, but decided to work anyway.

Finally, one day after work, I saw my doctor.

I was glad I didn't call in sick. Instead, I arranged to take a personal day.

Sometimes calling in sick is the right thing to do. Visit your doctor, sleep-in, watch TV, listen to music, make it a fiesta.

If possible, avoid calling in sick. The result? You'll develop a reputation as a reliable and committed employee.

1. Take care of yourself.
2. Call in sick when necessary.
3. Meditate on the nature of your illness. What one thing can you learn? Make it a healing of the mind as well as your body.

Taking Care Of Yourself Is Good Therapy

- Pop Culture: Moyers, Bill. *Healing and the Mind.* New York: Doubleday, 1993.

Take A Spa Day

When the stress of everyday life begins to wear me down, I build myself back up. I take a personal day and create my own holiday.

I'll go swimming; have a pedicure and a massage. To successfully manage stress, is to successfully manage one's life.

Remember…to stop and smell the petunia-begonias.

1. What's your favorite way to relax?
2. How do you feel after a massage? A pedicure?
3. Design your own spa day.

Rejuvenation Is Good Therapy

- Pop Culture: McKay, Mathew, Sutker, Catherine, Beck. *The Self-Nourishment Companion.* Oakland, CA: New Harbinger Publications, Inc, 2001.

Money

Your best investment is in yourself. The better you take care of yourself, the better you'll be able to take care of others.

How do you invest in yourself? Have faith in your dreams, ideas, and passions.

One of the best investments I ever made is joining a health club. The cost is ten dollars per month. Granted, one doesn't need a health club to stay physically fit, but I love to swim. It's also close to home, has free give-aways, convenient hours and interesting people watching.

The first rule of finance is, to pay yourself first. Put ten dollars or a hundred, into a savings account each month.

I like to pay rock-bottom prices. Matinees, vintage stores and low-cost haircuts (Usama Hair Design on State). It's fun to be creative. Think of ways you can save money. Have a yard sale, go on e-bay, or start a business. Everyone is good at something.

Your best investment is in yourself.

Paying Yourself First Is Good Therapy

- Pop Culture: Orman, Suze. *The Courage to Be Rich*. New York: Riverhead Books, 1999.

Rock-Bottom

Living rock-bottom style is a state of mind. It's champagne living at sparkling cider prices.

Do you like sales, discounts and vintage stores?

I like to make the most of what I have. Spend less, have more. When on a budget, you are forced to be creative about your time, money and resources.

My apartment is small, but inexpensive. I love the location, nearby transportation, Lincoln Park, health club, restaurants, bookstores and movie houses.

1. What's important in your world?
2. How can you save money?
3. Could you be happy spending less?

Living Rock-Bottom Is Good Therapy

- Pop Culture: Roman, Sanaya, Packer, Duane. *Creating Money.* Tiburon, CA: H J Kramer, Inc, 1988.

Happy Shirt

I have a navy blue, white and yellow floral shirt. It's polyester, long-sleeved with a wide collar, vintage 1970's. It always puts a smile on my face. How can you be sad when you put your happy shirt on?

Sometimes I don't like my job. Wearing my happy shirt makes my day. Do you have a favorite piece of clothing? Spend some time at a vintage or thrift shop. It could make your day. Put your happy shirt on.

1. How do colors affect your mood?
2. Do you feel better when you're dressed up?
3. How does what you wear affect others?

Happy Clothes Are Good Therapy

- Pop Culture: Hartman, Taylor. *The Color Code*. New York: Scribner, 1998.

A Million Dollars

What would you do, if you had a million dollars? Would you quit your job, buy a boat, sail around the world? Pretend as if you were a millionaire, and think about how your life would be different.

It's possible that some of the things you want can be accomplished without a million in the bank. Give yourself the luxury to start living richly, within your means. Go to a health spa or get a massage. Redecorate. Buy some flowers.

Vacation days are my currency.

1. What would you do with a million dollars? Ten Million?
2. Does money create happiness?
3. Do something you love the money will follow. True or false?

Living Richly Is Good Therapy

- Pop Culture: Sinetar, Marsha. *Do What You Love, the Money Will Follow*. New York: Dell Trade Paperback, 1987.

California

After graduating from college, I moved to Vista. I worked as an order clerk for a small food distributor, sold consumer electronics at a department store, and as a caterer. Spent time with my two Aunts. Visited San Diego, Los Angeles, Coronado and Diamond Bar in a Pacer. I met new people, learned about life. California was a grand adventure.

Six months later, I moved back to Chicago, homesick for the Midwest, my sister and mother.

Travel Is Good Therapy

- Pop Culture: Stoddard, Alexander. *Daring to be Yourself.* New York: Avon Books, 1990.

St. Louis

After a short-lived marriage, I decided to move to St. Louis.

Living in Soulard, I was a hostess, a Real Estate Agent and a front desk assistant at a health club, folding 400 towels a shift. People in St. Louis were very friendly. I was on Prozac the whole time.

Adventure Is Good Therapy

- Pop Culture: *The Wizard of Oz* (1939).

Show Me A Sign, In The Show Me State

I'd been living in St. Louis about a year. I was getting discouraged. I asked the universe to please "show me a sign".

My shift at the health club began at 5:30 a.m. on the lower level of a building in the center of downtown. Unlocking the doors to the health club, several regulars were lined up each day.

In addition to folding towels, I registered new members and answered the phone.

One day, at the end of my shift, a member came in. I barely knew him.

It turns out he was a florist. He gave me two dozen pink tea roses, tied with a raffia bow, standing in a gold dish. The card had an angel on it, and in it, he thanked me for being so cheerful, so early in the morning.

Asking Questions Is Good Therapy

• Pop Culture: MacLaine, Shirley. *Going Within*. New York: Bantam, 1989.

53

Insomnia

Sometimes I wake up in the middle of the night. Often this means my soul is sending me a message. Literally, to wake up.

For example, something was amiss. It was my "second" job. Working for a small company didn't feel right. I was in the midst of training for a new position.

The money was generous but my heart wasn't in it. After weighing my options, I told the CEO I would not be accepting the promotion.

She asked if she had done anything wrong.

"No, the position isn't right for me. I will be staying on Wall Street."

I slept through the night. Insomnia had sent me a signal. Message transmitted and received. Listen to your body. It may be sending you a message.

Sometimes an increase in salary or a change of scenery looks good on paper, but does not feel right. It's your life. Do what makes you happy.

1. Do you have trouble sleeping through the night?
2. Is there a problem at work? Home?
3. Consider your options. Talk to a friend.

Listening To Your Soul Is Good Therapy

- Pop Culture: Northrup, Christine. *Women's Bodies, Women's Wisdom.* New York: Bantam, 1998.

Words, Words, Words

At a party, I told someone I was on Prozac. I was taking 40 mg a day instead of my usual twenty, and was unwittingly following my bliss.

Moments later, the hostess took me aside and quietly told me to stop telling anyone at the party I took Prozac.

True, there is a time and place for everything.

Start a dialogue about Prozac, depression and anxiety. Not at work or at a party, but with family, friends and especially with yourself.

Stand up and say *PROZAC! PROZAC! PROZAC!*

Take your power back. There's no shame in depression, it's the number one disease in the world.

Use depression as a tool for self-discovery. Like life, it's a gift. Learn from your sadness, be kind to yourself and continue on your journey.

1. Why are you sad?
2. What can you do to improve your life?
3. Take baby steps.

Being Open Is Good Therapy

- Pop Culture: Bradshaw, John: *Healing The Shame That Binds You.* Deerfield Beach, FL: Health Communications, Inc,1988.

Drug Awareness

In fifth grade, much emphasis was placed on drug awareness, the illegal street variety. No one mentioned *prescription drug awareness.*

Educate yourself about anti-depressants. Get a second opinion.

As a doctor was re-filling my umpteenth prescription for Prozac, I told him it made me "feel good."

He said meditation could have the same effect.

I told him I couldn't meditate regularly. Didn't have the patience. Didn't have the time. Years later, I realized he was right.

Meditation, exercise and prayer all work for me. Taking care of myself is my responsibility. The healing process takes time.

Patience Is Good Therapy

- Pop Culture: Selby, John, von Luhmann. *Conscious Healing.* New York,: Bantam,!991.

Criticism

"You're just looking for love."

"You're immature."

"You're a socializer."

I've been told all of the above. I think we're all looking for love to a certain degree. The great love. Puppy love. Love of family and friends. Maybe this person meant I should love myself more. Tag, I'm it.

When someone told me I was immature and socializing too much, I thought maybe I should give seminars on claiming your Inner Child. Everyone's a critic. Use criticism as an opportunity to learn. Often there's a grain of truth in every criticism.

Being Kind And Loving Is Good Therapy

- Pop Culture: Stone, Hal, & Stone, Sidra. *Embracing Your Inner Critic.* New York: HarperSanFrancisco, 1993.

Love

What is love to you?

I love my sisters, my cousins, my family and friends, my home, writing and playing volleyball at the beach as the sun is setting on a summer day in Chicago.

Love is discipline. Setting limits. Being kind. Helpful. Paying attention. Love is joy.

What is love to you?

Love Is Good Therapy

• Pop Culture: Jampolsky, Gerald, G. *Love Is Letting Go of Fear.* Berkeley,CA: Celestial Arts, 1979.

Act Like You're In Love

When you're in love, everything tastes better, feels better, looks better, and sounds better.

Practice being in love. Be in love with life. It doesn't cost anything. You don't need a specific person, job or possession to be in love. It's an attitude. You have everything you need.

Act like you're in love. See what happens.

Being In Love With Life Is Good Therapy

- Pop Culture: Buscaglia, Leo. *LOVE.* New York: Fawcett Crest Book, 1972.

Summer In The City

o o o o o o o o o o o o o o o o o o o o o o o o o o o o o o o o
North Avenue Beach
Sun was hot and new
on my city-born skin
We drove by motorcycle
mid-afternoon
to catch a few beams.
My suit yellow blue and green
fresh from K-mart
He in long lime trunks
Lying on a quiet paradise
Side by side
quietly murmuring
softly sleeping
then a little Reiki,
frisbee
summer ends too soon.

Write a poem about love or adventure. Or anything. It's fun to express yourself
in different ways.

Self-Expression Is Good Therapy

• Pop Culture: Goldberg, Natalie. *Writing Down the Bones.* Boston, MA: Shambhala Publications, 1986.

Fears

I'm afraid. Of everything. Waking up. Taking a shower. Getting dressed. Going to work. Being on time. Making a mistake. Getting criticized. Getting in trouble.

In spite of this, I go to work everyday. Pay my bills. And do an Irish jig. Sometimes you have to put one foot in front of the other. Face your fears one at a time. Eventually, they'll lose their grip.

1. What are you afraid of?
2. Why?
3. What can you do about it?

Facing Your Fears Is Good Therapy

- Pop Culture: Hallowell, Edward M. *Worry.* New York: Ballantine Book, 1997.

Feeling Good

"Most folks are as happy as they make up their minds to be."

—*Abraham Lincoln*

After a good night's sleep, I'll go to the health club, swim a few laps, eat lunch and feel like a million. This is a natural high. I will feel so good, I'll wonder, "Why are some people so unhappy?"

My father often said, "People are frustrated, never let them know how happy you are." Life is a series of choices. Sometimes I get discouraged. Then, when I'm tired of suffering, I do something about it. Meditate, count my blessings, give thanks to the universe and make a plan. Do something.

It's important to take care of yourself. Go swimming, jog, or take a walk around the block. Feel good about feeling good.

Feeling Good Is Good Therapy

• Pop Culture: Burns, David, D. *Feeling Good*. New York: Avon Books, 1992.

Feelings

o o o o o o o o o o o o o o o o o o o o o o o o o o o o o o o o o
"No one can make you feel inferior, without your consent"

—*Eleanor Roosevelt*

Feelings come and go like the tide.

Honor your feelings because they are messages from your soul. If you're happy, ask yourself why? When you're sad, ask why?

Once you begin to understand the language of your feelings, you begin to understand and appreciate yourself. Feelings are nothing to be afraid of, or ashamed of.

To be alive is to have feelings.

Feelings Are Good Therapy

• Pop Culture: Gaylin, Willard. *Feelings.* New York: Ballantine Books, 1979.

Doctors

I had a new family doctor. He had a boyish face. And was a few years younger than me.

He knew I had broken up with someone and was sad. I was looking for moral support. I was living life without a crutch. Life without Prozac.

My doctor didn't like the guy. I started crying. I said I had joined a writing class.

His reply to my tears, "There are some very good drugs on the market I can prescribe. I've successfully treated hundreds of patients."

"No thank-you," I said. "I've been down that route."

He knew I had taken Prozac before.

"How much writing have you been getting done?"

He was taunting me now, like a bully on the playground. Perhaps he was treating me the only way he knew. I had been on a crying jag and he had just the drug to cure me. Getting over a broken heart isn't easy. But it can be done. For the heart to fully heal, one must take time to grieve.

I took time to heal. I also joined a new medical group and found a much better doctor.

Doctors aren't perfect they're only human.

The Right Doctor Is Good Therapy

- Pop Culture: Ponder, Catherine. *The Dynamic Laws of Healing.* Marina del Rey, CA: DeVorss & Company, 1985.

Tears

I have a Ph.D. in crying. Sometimes I'm sad, frustrated, or just depressed. Sometimes it's PMS. Sometimes, I think I'm crying about one thing, when I'm really upset about something else.

Tears are Mother Nature's way of releasing toxins and pent-up emotions. One day I have everything figured out, the next day, I'm clueless. Progress is two steps back and one step forward.

Tears are nothing to be ashamed of. It's best not to cry at work, but in the privacy of your own home. Cry long enough, and eventually you'll get tired, and things will look brighter.

Work through the pain. Call a friend. Go for a walk. Keep your chin up.

Tears are OK.

Crying Is Good Therapy

• Pop Culture: *Broadcast News* (1987).

Grief

Everyone grieves. It's part of life. Death, divorce, break-ups, disappointment, there's no escaping hardship.

I got married on Zoloft and divorced on Prozac. At my father's deathbed, I was also on medication. I have photos of me smiling broadly, shortly before he passed on.

Years after my divorce and father's death, I mourned the loss of my marriage, my father and my heart's desire at the same time. Perhaps prescription drugs interfered with the initial grieving process.

Ironically, my father was against Prozac.

He said to "Take vitamins and exercise everyday."

I was too stubborn. I was determined to do things my way.

About a year after he died, like a baby gives up the bottle, I gave up Prozac for good. It's good to be in the driver's seat again.

Grieving Is Good Therapy

- Pop Culture: Welshons, John, E. *Awakening from Grief.* Little Falls, NJ: Open Heart Publications, 2000.

What The Policeman Told Me

I had a new primary doctor. I told him I'd like to speak to a counselor. He said he, and his medical group were anti-talk therapy. I told him I had a lot of things on my mind and would like to talk to someone. He said he would be unable to help me.

After I burst into tears, he said OK, but I'd have to fill out a questionnaire and had better answer all the questions as if I were borderline suicidal.

When I arrived home, his receptionist called and said she had the fax number for the referral. I said I'd prefer a phone number.

She called back with the number.

I called. It was a hospital. A woman asked for my social security number and other personal data. I told her I wanted to make an appointment to see a counselor. She said she was going off-duty, but I could make an appointment with the next operator.

The next woman also asked for my social security number and other personal information.

"No," again I replied. I wasn't on any medication.

She said she would be unable to make an appointment, and I would have to call back tomorrow. In a moment of protest, I decided to hang up.

A few minutes later, my doorbell rang. I wasn't expecting anyone, so I ignored it.

Then, there was a heavy knock at the door.

"Who's there?"

"The police, ma'am. You OK?"

There, outside my door, were Chicago's Finest. Two young, handsome policemen. God does deliver.

I told them I was fine. Then a veteran of the force arrived, with a paddy wagon. They told him I was fine and he left.

The two men in blue were in my third floor studio apartment.

"Don't you have an important drug deal to attend to?" I asked.

"No."

They wanted to know what was wrong. I told them I wanted to make an appointment. They said they'd be happy to talk to me, right now. We talked for half an hour and this is what one of the policemen told me:

1. Work on your resume.

2. Try bartending (they said cops don't make much, and they were looking for part-time work, also).

3. Call in sick, and go to Las Vegas for the weekend with friends.

Later, I thought about the policeman and wanted to thank him. One night, I was doing my laundry. Jaywalking towards the Laundromat, I saw a police car and looked in. He smiled, and I told him I'm doing much better.

Talking Is Good Therapy

• Pop Culture: Monaghan, Patricia. *Office Oracle*. St. Paul, MN: Llewellyn Publications, 1999.

Uncle Frank

My Uncle Frank is a great conversationalist. Sometimes we talk for hours and it seems only minutes have passed. He is an even better listener.

Uncle Frank is from the great state of Tennessee. In college, he was class president.

Years ago, he was experiencing anxiety. His doctor gave him a prescription, good for one week only.

"That's all," the doctor said, "I want you to think about what's bothering you."

He did think about what was bothering him. No more drugs were needed or given. We all have problems, difficulties, and stress.

If I have a problem, I know I can call my Uncle Frank.

Uncle Frank Is Good Therapy

- Pop Culture: Ponder, Catherine. *The Dynamic Laws of Prosperity.* Marina del Rey, CA: Devorss & Company, 1985.

My Dentist

My dentist is an upbeat fellow. He always tells me to *"Stay away from negative people."*

We're both film buffs. Steve McQueen, Paul Newman and Robert DeNiro are three of his favorite actors. He likes to talk about the good time he had in Guadalajara, Mexico, when they were filming *Circus of the Stars* with Suzanne Somers and John Ritter.

One day an acquaintance suggested I change real estate companies. She knew someone in the business. She said I should buy a car, also.

I told her I made a large commission selling a property a few blocks from home and having a car had nothing to do with it.

She said, "That was a fluke."

My reply, "When my book becomes successful, are you going to say that's a fluke, too?"

She was speechless.

Like my dentist says, "Stay away from negative people." Some people, places and things are negative and some are positive. Be careful whom you associate with. Stay away from negative people. They'll suck the life out of you.

Positive People Are Good Therapy

- Pop Culture: Bernstein, Albert J. *Emtional Vampires*. New York: McGraw-Hill, 2001.

Accept Yourself

Once I had a wart on my face. My doctor removed it with liquid nitrogen. He then burned a match and made a black mole-like shape. Looking in the mirror, I smiled; an ugly wart became a glamorous Marilyn Monroe-like temporary mole.

Accepting yourself means liking yourself warts and all. Whether you have a wart on your face or the hair of a troll, learn to love your body and it will love you back. Be kind to yourself.

1. Do you like your body?
2. How do you feel about your body, after you exercise?
3. How does being kind improve your life?

Accepting Yourself Is Good Therapy

- Pop Culture: Ray, Sondra. *Loving Relationships*. Berkeley, CA: Celestial Arts, 1980.

Write Your Own Affirmations

o o o o o o o o o o o o o o o o o o o o o o o o o o o o o o o o
I'm healthy.
I'm wealthy.
I'm strong.

Create your own affirmations. Saying positive things helps you to create your own reality.

Saying negative words can be useful too, because you are taking their power away. Try, *Loser, Loser, Loser,* like my co-worker does. I can't help but feel better after saying that.

When you embrace aspects of yourself you don't like, you become powerful. We are all unique human beings. Rich, poor, short or tall, there's no one just like you.

1. List some affirmations.
2. List some things you like about yourself.
3. List some things you don't like about yourself.

Affirmations Are Good Therapy

• Pop Culture: Steinem, Gloria. *Revolution From Within.* Little, Brown and Company, 1992.

Bill of Rights

I have had a great need to please others, to be popular, to be pretty. It seemed necessary to earn my "right" to be here. We all have a "right" to be here. Being born is our ticket to admission.

When you like and approve of yourself, you begin to lose the need for votes. Start liking yourself and take your power back. Devise your own Bill of Rights, uniquely suited to your needs and desires.

By writing things down, you develop clarity of mind and purpose. You can't help anyone until you help yourself first.

1. It's OK to take care of yourself.
2. It's OK to pray.
3. It's OK to stand up for yourself and others.
4. It's OK to help others, within reason.
5. It's OK to embrace your "shadow" side.
6. It's OK to pursue your dreams.
7. It's OK to put your needs first.
8. It's OK to ask for what you want.
9. It's OK to avoid negative people, places and things.
10. It's OK to believe in the mystery and power of the universe.

Standing Up For Yourself Is Good Therapy

- Pop Culture: Beattie, Melody. *Codependent No More*. Center City, MN: Hazelden, 1992

Book Therapy

I love to read. Reading is healing. When you read the stories of other people's lives, you're able to transcend your own difficulties. We're all connected.

Three books I highly recommend:

1. Russell Baker. *Growing Up.* New York: Congdon & Weed, Inc, 1982.
2. Thomas Moore. *Care of the Soul.* New York: HarperPerennial, 1992.
3. Louise L. Hay. *You Can Heal Your Life.* Carson, CA: Hay House, Inc, 1984.

Books are my passion. New and used, funny, sad, inspiring, art, health, wealth and show business books, I love to read.

Reading improves your mind. Knowledge is wealth. Browse second hand stores, yard sales, or start a book club with friends. A library card is an excellent way to read for free, rock-bottom style.

Reading Is Good Therapy

• Pop Culture: Bratman, Steven. *Health Food Junkies.* New York: Broadway Books, 2000.

Movie Therapy

Watching films can heal, inspire and uplift. In a fog over a break-up, I rented *The Way We Were* starring Barbra Streisand. As the film progressed I felt better about my romantic tribulations, because Barbra was suffering too. Movies have the power to heal your soul. Make a snack, sit back and go to the movies today.

Three favorites:

1. *East of Eden* (1955).
2. *About A Boy* (2002).
3. *It's a Wonderful Life* (1946).

Movies Are Good Therapy

- Pop Culture: Biskind, Peter. *Easy Riders, Raging Bulls.* New York: Simon & Schuster, 1998.

Music Therapy

"Music soothes the savage beast" is a popular expression. I know this is true for me. Music improves my mood.

I like the Beatles, Madonna, and Nirvana. No Doubt, Sugar Ray and the Tom Tom Club. Music can tune your soul.

If I'm feeling blue, I turn on the radio. Within minutes, I feel better. A little music and my faith in humanity is restored.

My dad was from Mexico. He liked Fleetwood Mac, The Doors, and Pete Seeger's, *Guantanamera*. What music would you choose for the soundtrack of your life? Rock? Jazz, country or classical? Music can inspire, motivate and heal.

1. What is your favorite type of music?
2. Do you like to sing?
3. Play a musical instrument?

Music Is Good Therapy

- Pop Culture: *Pete Seeger-Clearwater Classics.* Sony Music Special Products, 1993.

Be Prepared

"Know your lines, know your mark, and be on time."

—*Cary Grant*

Serendipity is fun. Being prepared is better. So I buy Christmas cards, books and gifts in advance. Plan my wardrobe for the week. Make a list. Stock up on groceries. Whenever I leave for work ten minutes early my whole day seems to go better.

You can never be fully prepared for life's emergencies. It helps to be flexible, find a middle ground and do your best.

Being prepared primes you for future success. Steps taken today can meet with opportunity tomorrow.

1. How do you like to prepare?
2. Make a list of important birthdays and anniversaries.
3. Get a new telephone/address book and update.

Being Prepared Is Good Therapy

• Pop Culture: Emmett, Rita. *The Procrastinator's Handbook.* New York: Walker & Company, 2000.

When You've Outgrown A Friend

Friendships offer comfort and joy. Sometimes you've outgrown a friend and need to move on. How do you know when it's over? Perhaps you've grown apart. Have different interests. It can be a gnawing feeling of discontent.

I had a friend for over a decade. I am grateful for the good times we had. When I was no longer comfortable sharing my hopes and dreams, I knew it was over.

For example, at the dawn of a New Year, I said I'd like to write a book, get married and have a baby.

Her reply, "Why don't you have a baby now? My husband and I can help you."

They lived a state away. She disapproved of the object of my affections. She was egging me on to be a mom before I was established, in my career or relationship. Soon after, I distanced myself from her.

Sometimes you've outgrown a friend. Just let go. A feeling of peace was my reward. Take control of your life. Move on from people or situations that are no longer right for you.

Moving On Is Good Therapy

• Pop Culture: Ullmann, Liv. *Changing.* New York: Bantam Book, 1978.

Good Things

Everyone experiences hard times and stress. Whenever I start feeling sorry for myself, I mentally make a list of my "wins". Feeling sorry for yourself takes your power away.

Anyone can add their losses and sorrows. Choose to look at things from a different perspective. Focus on the good things. Add up your wins, no matter how small. Had a good day at work. Caught the early train. Was kind to people. Got a raise.

Make a list of all the positives in your life. This is the equivalent of doing push-ups for your psyche. We are all responsible for building a stronger mind, body and soul.

A "Win" List Is Good Therapy

- Pop Culture: Peck, M. Scott. *The Road Less Traveled.* New York: Touchstone, 1978.

You Don't Need Anything

You don't "need" anything. My mom and Uncle Frank taught me this powerful concept. I thought, maybe I needed a husband. Needed Prozac. Needed this, or that, to be complete.

Whether you're single or married, it doesn't matter. Both have their virtues. The secret is to enjoy whatever stage of life you're in.

You are a complete person on your own. Whenever you think you "need" something, it begins to own you. You're no longer free. You're a jailbird. Become your own person. Find the joy in all you do.

Being Independent Is Good Therapy

• Pop Cultue: *The Shawshank Redemption (1994).*

Make The Most Of...

I have met a lot of people at work: young parents, students, a dentist, a grandfather, and a soccer mom.

Made a few friends and many acquaintances. Have medical and dental insurance and a 401-k. These are some of the unwritten and written benefits of the job.

While working, I make the most of my job and environment. Sometimes that's all you can do. We're all surrounded by opportunities. The secret is to *"make the most of wherever you are."*

1. List your work benefits.
2. How could you make the most of these?
3. What changes would you like? Flexible hours, over-time, a salary increase?

Making The Most of...Is Good Therapy

• Pop Culture: King, Serge Kahili. *Urban Shaman.* New York: Fireside, 1990.

Everything I Need To Know I Learned In the Pits

I work on Wall Street in Chicago. As a clerk, I deliver orders to buy and sell all day in the pits. Life on the trading floor can be hurricane fast or painstakingly slow. This is what I've learned:

Respect your elders
Be assertive
Get to the point
Be courteous
Listen
Pay attention
One order at a time
Wait your turn
Don't hold grudges
Time is money
Have fun.

Because of the fever pitch and intensity of trading, tempers flare, papers fly, words are exchanged, but you can't stay mad, because it's just business and we'll all be back tomorrow. Like a family.

Work Is Good Therapy

• Pop Culture: *Wall Street* (1987).

Intuition

I work a few hours a week in an office. I file and make copies. Going home at four o'clock, I'd begun to notice a bar/restaurant named Stocks and Blondes, under the "L".

I thought I should go in there one day. But never did.

Time passes and I see my sister. She tells me her eldest stepson, works at Stocks and Blondes.

It's easy to ignore your inner voice, promptings or feelings. The more you pay attention to the quiet voice inside, the better you'll be at receiving messages.

Trust your intuition. You never know where it will lead you.

1. What does intuition mean to you?
2. Recall a time you listened to your inner voice.
3. What is your intuition telling you? To call a friend, join a club, or take the day off?

Listening to your Intuition Is Good Therapy

• Pop Culture: Gawain, Shatki. *Living in the Light.* Mill Valley, CA: Whatever Publishing, 1986.

Secret Santa

It was Final's Week, my second year of college in the Dorm. We all gave and received small gifts for a "Secret Santa" week. I don't remember the gifts, but I remember the notes I received. They went something like this:

> *Dear Eva,*
> *You've been studying hard for your finals, and will do well.*
>
> *Day Two,*
> *Good luck on your tests, you're very smart.*
>
> *Day Three,*
> *Santa has been watching you and knows what a hard-worker you are. Enjoy your Winter Break you deserve it.*

I was truly amazed at her kind and uplifting words. Good words are good therapy. Write your own letter of encouragement. Or give one to a friend. Like a plant needs water and sunshine, we all enjoy words of positive praise.

Letters Of Encouragement Are Good Therapy

• Pop Culture: Conari Press, The editors of. *More Random Acts of Kindness.* Berkeley, CA: Conari Press, 1994.

Thank-You Notes

Thank-you notes are letters of appreciation and gratitude. Writing a letter of thanks only takes a few moments. A note written on colorful stationery or a postcard is a thoughtful way to show you care.

A few samples:

> *Dear Jessica,*
> *Thank-you. Your help is greatly appreciated. We had a lot of fun. Good luck in school and all your after-school activities.*
> *Love, Auntie Eva*
> *P.S. I'm still sorting!*

> *Dear Donna,*
> *Thank you for your kindness. Please know your graceful ways are admired. You're always there with a kind word. You are a "star".*
> *Sincerely, Eva*

> *Dear Julie,*
> *Thank-you for the wonderful gifts. I love the cosmetic bags and all the make-up. They make saying good-bye to summer easier.*
> *Your friend, Eva*

> *Thank-You Notes Are Good Therapy*

- Pop Culture: Mathews, Andrew. *Making Friends.* Los Angeles, CA: Price Stern Sloan, 1991.

Smooth It Over

Whether it's in my personal or business life, I've learned it's best to smooth things over.

Write a thank-you note or make that follow up phone call. Let the people in your life know they're important to you.

After a summer visit in Chicago, my father was on his way home to Puerto Vallarta. We got into an argument, right before his three thousand-mile journey.

He called from Texas. He'd been in a car accident. He was OK.

Try to smooth things over in your life. Make that call, tell someone you're sorry, you'll both be better off.

Making Amends Is Good Therapy

- Pop Culture: Mathews, Andrew. *Being Happy.* Los Angeles, CA: Price Stern Sloan, 1990.

Turn A Negative Into A Positive

o o o o o o o o o o o o o o o o o o o o o o o o o o o o o o o o
"Things are neither good nor bad but thinking makes them so."

—Shakespeare

Due to cutbacks, my overtime was reduced. At first I was upset. I liked the extra money. Then a positive thought occurred to me. Working less gave me more time to write.

I was also getting "stressed" by the long hours and needed time to exercise. Instead of being unhappy, I chose to see the positive. Every negative can be turned into a positive.

1. List three things you don't like about your life.
2. Can any of these situations be changed?
3. If not, can you change your thinking or attitude? Say yes, and you'll be a STAR.

Seeing The Positive Is Good Therapy

• Pop Culture: Peck, M. Scott. *The Road Less Traveled and Beyond.* New York: Simon And Schuster, 1997.

Top Ten Quick Fixes

If you're feeling blue or unmotivated, try the following:

1. Look at your baby picture.
2. Write a thank-you note.
3. Tell a joke.
4. Make a plan.
5. Paint a picture.
6. Listen to music.
7. Call a friend.
8. Take a walk.
9. Make a grateful list.
10. Life rewards action.

Taking Action Is Good Therapy

- Pop Culture: *Billy Madison* (1995).

Write A Few Words

A journal can be a useful tool. You can list the things that give you joy. You can list the things that give you pain. You can write about your medical experiences. A journal can be about whatever you want.

For example:

I dreamt that scientist's say we eat parts of cockroaches and even rats-because they're in our home. There were hundreds of roaches that couldn't be seen close-up, and they were leaving droppings everywhere—(unable for us to see) and they were harboring themselves behind walls. A scientist said he went behind the walls with a video camera and saw them.

Yes, I was on Prozac at the time.

A Journal Is Good Therapy

* Pop Culture: Mooyaart, B. M, Translated From the Dutch by. *Anne Frank: The Diary of a Young Girl.* New York: Pocket Books, 1953.

Winning Qualities

Make a list of your winning qualities. Writing this list reminds you of your good points.

1. Reliable
2. Caring friend
3. Good sense of humor
4. Athletic
5. Well-read
6. Flexible
7. Open
8. Perseveres
9. Intelligent
10. Loves kids

Being Positive Is Good Therapy

- Pop Culture: Viscott, David. *Winning.* New York: Pocket Books, 1972.

- Pop Culture: Viscott, David. *Emotional Resilience.* New York: Harmony Books, 1996.

Always Have A Plan

Before making a telephone call, I like to make a list of key points I want to communicate.

This way, I won't forget something important.

If I'm going somewhere, I like to have a plan. What are my goals? What are my objectives? What do I bring to the party? What time do I want to leave? How do I get there? Where are the exits? Life is easier when you have a plan. Life doesn't always work out the way you want it to. That's why it's good to have a plan. It's a starting point.

Having A Plan Is Good Therapy

- Pop Culture: Sarno, John E. *Healing Back Pain.* New York: Warner Books, 1991.

Take Pictures

My sister Ingrid and her husband John had a Memorial Day party. I suggested a Hawaiian theme. Several people wore Hawaiian shirts and a neighbor brought some Don Ho records.

I wasn't in a party mood. But I showed up. I had a camera and took pictures. A month later, I gave my sister a small photo album.

I'm glad I went to the party. It was fun to see the different Hawaiian shirts. It was fun to take pictures. Sometimes the best thing in life is to just show up.

Showing Up Is Good Therapy

- Pop Culture: Cameron, Julia. *The Artist's Way*. New York: A Jeremy Tarcher/ Putnam Book, 1992.

Adventures In Therapy

I called Dr. K to make our first appointment.

I told her I had not yet received the proper authorization papers from my doctor. She said that was no problem, we'll work that out later. Dr. K was in private practice.

"Another therapist, was this necessary?" I wondered, than recalled it was my idea. She said to take "very good care" before hanging up.

During our 50-minute session, we discussed events from the past. About midway she said, "I'd like to confer with your doctor about your treatment."

I was surprised, because my doctor wasn't treating me for anything. Too many cooks spoil the soup.

Dr. K asked me what I wanted out of therapy. I told her I wanted someone to add to my support system. She did not reply.

At the end of the session she asked when I'd like my next appointment. I said in three weeks.

Looking alarmed, she asked "Why the delay?"

My response, "I'm working over-time, my birthday is approaching, my mother will be visiting, and I'd like to go swimming."

EUREKA! If you're busy living, you don't need to sit on a couch. Unless it's in your own home, relaxing, after a full day of working, playing, and humming- all the ingredients of a happy life.

She wanted me there every week like clockwork. Before five and not on weekends. Said that's the way she operated.

Suddenly, I felt much better. My friends, family and even my co-workers were all part of my support system. Therapy is good if you need it, if not, let it go.

1. See a therapist if necessary.
2. Don't be intimidated by a counselor. They're working for you. Interview more than one.
3. Consider talking to a supportive friend or family member.

Letting Go Is Good Therapy

- Pop Culture: Lewis, Richard. *The Other Great Depression.* New York: Public Affairs, 2000.

More On Being Sensitive

As a little girl, my Aunt Joan told me I was sensitive. She said I was like her, and took things to heart. I can see how being sensitive can make you more likely to turn to "something" to kill the pain.

In college, a psychiatrist was assigned to me, to see if I was "lying" about my physical symptoms.

He said I probably wasn't lying, just "histrionic". Seems some doctors are afraid if you are remotely theatrical.

Doctors are limited, they can perform tests, prescribe medication and can encourage you to take better care of yourself. You are responsible for a healthy mind, body and soul. You have to take care of yourself.

Make it a priority. I always feel better when I exercise, meditate, eat right and get my rest.

See your friends, listen to the radio, and surround yourself with positive people, places and things. Being sensitive is OK.

Taking Care is Good Therapy

- Pop Culture: Fulghum, Robert. *All I Really Need to Know I Learned in Kindergarten.* New York: Ivy Books, 1989.

Forgive

I realized I remember things people say. Not so nice things.

It's easy to nurse a grudge. It might be too late to repair the past, but it's never too late to forgive. It hurts to hold on.

Sometimes, people say things without thinking. They might be in pain.

Forgive, and you free your soul. You'll be lighter. Drop the heavy baggage.

I forgave my Dad. He was in pain. He took it out on me.

When I got older, he said he didn't want to discuss it. I forgave him and we moved on.

Start a new life. Forgive.

What angers you, owns you. Write down any hurts and resentments, and then let it go. Kiss it good-bye. Make a decision to move on and get on with your life.

1. Who do you need to forgive?
2. How do you feel after you forgive?
3. Remember to forgive yourself.

Forgiveness Is Good Therapy

• Pop Culture: Keyes, Jr, Ken. *The Power of Unconditional Love.* Coos Bay, OR: Love Line Books, 1990.

Rock Me Boom-Boom, Mor-Mor

Mor-mor means mother's mother in Swedish. Growing up, my grandparents Mor-mor and John-Eric lived downstairs and we lived upstairs. Everyone needs a safe haven. Mine was my grandmother.

"Rock me boom-boom, Mor-mor," I'd say, and she would rock me in her arms singing, "Boom-boom, Boom-boom."

As we get older, we must develop our inner resources for comfort. Meditation helps me find that place. A memory, or a few moments spent in quiet reflection allow you to connect with your spirit. Feed your soul with meditation and rock your world, boom-boom.

1. Take a meditation class.
2. Spend quiet time reflecting.
3. Write your thoughts in a notebook.

Reflection Is Good Therapy

• Pop Culture: Goldstein, Joan and Soares Manuela. *The Joy Within*. A Beginner's Guide to Meditation. New York: Fireside, 1990.

TMI

"Discretion is the better part of valor."

—*Falstaff in* King Henry the Fourth, Part One, *by William Shakespeare.*

Sometimes a person may share more details than you need to know. Personal details, financial details, or romantic details (too much information).

Whether this is a friend, a neighbor or a supervisor, remember to maintain your boundaries. Just because someone gives you bon mots about their personal life, doesn't mean you need to overshare also. Why? First, the other person may not care. Second, you will command more power, respect and sanity if you keep personal information to yourself.

Adopt a business like attitude in life and keep personal details to a minimum. A happy byproduct-you'll create mystery.

1. Write in a journal.
2. Talk to a family member.
3. Be mysterious.

Discretion Is Good Therapy

• Pop Culture: Love, Patricia with Robinson, Jo. *The Emotional Incest Syndrome.* New York: Bantam Books, 1990.

Options

Life is all about options. In every situation we have a choice.

It's up to us to exercise our options. The phone rings. I'm typing. Do I have to answer the phone? No. I could answer it, or let my voice mail pick up.

Sometimes it's a telemarketer. Often I'm not interested, and politely say no thank-you. Once I said yes to a credit card. Later I regretted having an extra card. I considered my options. Decided to save my money, and wrote a check for the balance.

We all have options. Use them wisely.

Options Are Good Therapy

- Pop Culture: Stoddard, Alexandra. *Making Choices*. New York: William Morrow and Company, 1994.

How To Swear With Savvy

I try not to swear. Occasionally, I do.

When my sister and I were not yet teen-agers, our mother let us swear. She didn't want us to be intimidated by those who did. Mom wasn't an advocate of foul language. She just wanted my sister and I to be savvy. She new in real life people swore.

Now, in the rare event I do swear, the people around me are in shock.

Being Savvy Is Good Therapy

- Pop Culture: Gordhamer, Soren. *Just Say Om!* Your Life's Journey. A Teenager's Guide. Avon, MA: Adams Media Corporation, 2001.

Simplify

I had a cell phone for two years. At the end of the contract, I gave it up. A land line was all I needed.

I used to work in a gift shop part-time in addition to working my day job and selling real estate. I gave up the gift shop.

When something no longer works for you, drop it like a hot potato. My life is so much better when I simplify. Less complicated. Less costly.

When you remove the unnecessary, you create time for the necessary. Do what's important to you, drop the rest.

What can you do to make your life simpler?

To Simplify Is Good Therapy

- Pop Culture: Kingston, Karen. *Clear Your Clutter with Feng Shui.* New York: Broadway Books, 1999.

Good Intentions

According to the dictionary, intent is purpose, aim. The state of mind with which an act is committed.

What is your intention? My aim is to write an uplifting, inspiring and entertaining story. When you become clear about what you want, reaching your goals becomes easier.

I choose to see the highest good in others and myself. This elevates the energy. Someone asked, "People are bad, how can you do that?"

My response, "I believe people are good. And when you choose to see the highest good in others you are often rewarded with their highest good."

Good Intentions Are Good Therapy

- Pop Culture: Kabat-Zinn, Jon. *Wherever You Go, There You Are.* New York: Hyperion, 1994.

Create A Nightly Ritual

At about nine in the evening, I stop answering the phone. I might take a relaxing bath or shower. Meditate for twenty minutes. And practice Reiki.

Other nights I may watch a late-night talk show. Laughter is good for the soul. Create your own ritual.

Relaxation is Good Therapy

- Pop Culture: Roman, Sanaya. *Soul Love*. Tiburon, CA: H J Kramer, 1997.

A Few Words From Dad

1. Be tranquil.
2. Don't add fuel to the fire.
3. You don't sound sick.
4. Be prepared.
5. Write a few words.
6. Save your money.
7. Buy real estate.
8. Establish yourself first.
9. Take vitamins.
10. Get off Prozac.

A Few Words Are Good Therapy

• Pop Culture: *Pretty in Pink* (1986).

Power Of Rock-Bottom

"Power is taken, not given."

—Murphy's Law

When you're at the bottom you've got nothing to lose. When you've got nothing to lose, you've got everything to gain. When I gave up Prozac, I asked myself, "What have I got to lose?" "My fancy job, husband or home?"

When I gave up Prozac, I gained everything. My soul, my integrity, my feelings, my pain, my grief, my sorrow, the good times and the bad. I got my life back.

Rock Bottom Is Good Therapy

- Pop Culture: Wilde, Stuart. *Silent Power*. Carlsbad, CA: Hay House, 1996.

0-595-32256-5